LEARN TO READ

Y0-BZV-138

planet earth

Bats

LEVEL 2

BOOK 9
long i
(igh, y)

by Quinlan B. Lee

ISBN-13: 978-0-545-14823-8
ISBN-10: 0-545-14823-5

12 11 10 9 8 7 6 5 4 3 2   9 10 11 12 13 14/0

Printed in China   95
First printing, September 2009

PHOTO CREDITS: COVER: ©Stephen Krasemann/Getty Images, Page 1: ©Four Oaks/Shutterstock,
Page 2: ©Chris Mattison/Alamy, Page 4: ©Maximilian Weinzierl/Alamy, Page 6: ©Images of Africa Photbank/Alamy,
Page 8: ©Imagebroker/Alamy, Page 10: ©Stephen Krasemann/Getty Images,
Page 12: ©The Natural History Museum/Alamy, Page 14: ©A & J Visage/Alamy

This is a big cave.

It is not **bright**.

There is very little **light**.

There is not a thing in **sight**.

Wait! Look up **high**.

What do you **spy**?

Do you **spy** a bat way up **high**?

What a **sight**!

There are more than one million bats!

They sleep up **high**.

They hang on **tight** with their claws.

They sleep all day and **fly** at **night**.

Night begins to fall.

The bats take **flight**.

A million bats **fly** out into

the **sky**.

Bats search for food at **night**.

Night is the **right** time to hunt for bugs.

Tonight, the bats will eat millions of bugs!

Bats do not **spy** bugs with their eyes.

It is hard to **spy** when there is no **light**.

They use sound instead of **sight**.

Sound helps them see at **night**.

Now the **night** fades.

Here comes the **light**.

The bats **fly** back to the cave.

Good **night**, bats.

Sleep **tight**.

Here are some facts for you to share:

- Caves are one of the least explored habitats on Earth. The caves that *have* been discovered are astonishing! The Cave of the Swallows in Mexico is deep enough for the Empire State Building to fit inside. Deer Cave in Borneo is large enough to fit a jumbo jet.

- Bats are everywhere! Bats live everywhere on Earth except the polar regions and some islands.

- Bats are the only mammals that fly. But unlike birds, their wings come out from their shoulders instead of their breast bones.

- Bats hunt insects using echolocation. They make a very loud cry that is so high, humans can't hear it and the sound waves reflect back from objects around the bat. The waves help them "see with sound" when it is too dark to see with their eyes.